Catching Your Breath in Grief

... and grace will lead you home

Every breath is precious.

Dom Atkins

Catching Your Breath in Grief

… and grace will lead you home

Thomas Attig

Photography by William L. Rathje

BREATH OF LIFE
PUBLISHING

BREATH OF LIFE
PUBLISHING

4 – 50 Dallas Road,
Victoria BC Canada V8V 1A2

For information and bulk orders, please contact:
Thomas Attig at tattigca@earthlink.net

To contact the author, go to tattigca@earthlink.
net or visit his web site at www.griefsheart.com.

Catching Your Breath in Grief:
and grace will lead you home
ISBN 978-0-9880760-0-6 (casebound)
ISBN 978-0-9880760-1-3 (trade paperback)
Cataloguing information available from
Library and Archives Canada.

Printed on acid-free paper.

10 9 8 7 6 5 4 3 2 1b

To my wife, Betty Davies,
for the grace of her caring soul and hopeful spirit.

And in memory of my dear friend, Bill Rathje,
who died before this work went to press.

CONTENTS

Part One—THE BREATH OF LIFE— 1

Part Two—WHEN LOSS TAKES YOUR BREATH AWAY—21

Part Three—CATCHING YOUR BREATH—35

PREFACE

When my Dad died over forty years ago, my young head filled with wonder. Where had the breath that sustained his life gone? Where had it come from? What was it like to realize he would soon breathe his last? Did he sense that he was saying good-bye to everything he ever knew or cared about? What did the flow of life through his seventy-three years mean to him, at the peaks and in the valleys? Why was I still breathing and he not? How had sharing twenty-four years changed us? What would my life be like without him? What would carry me through sorrow and crisis? What would dying be like for me one day? Why does anyone ever draw breath? Where does any individual life fit in the vastness of the universe?

I knew I was not alone in wondering about such matters. My Mom and brother were no doubt wondering, too, though I didn't know how to approach them. Sons and daughters, spouses and partners, parents and grandparents, and friends had been wondering as we were since humans first began to care about and love one another; grieve; reflect; engage with mysteries without and within; and express themselves in word, art, and ritual.

It is only human to wonder about an unseen "something more" that surrounds and holds us. And about an unseen "something more" deep within that enables us to transcend suffering, be at home, care and love, grow, strive, find faith and courage, hope, and thrive in death's shadow.

I have carried such wondering with me ever since Dad died. I wanted to share it with a reliable spiritual guide, but I doubted I knew any. I finished graduate studies and began teaching philosophy. My wondering moved me to introduce a course on death and dying, for students entering helping professions. I knew they would want wisdom about being with the dying and the bereaved. I knew I didn't have it, but I knew we could search together.

Over the years of reflecting on my own experiences; listening to stories of loss and sorrow; and wondering with so many students, survivors, family members, friends, teachers, researchers, and caregivers, I've become well acquainted with the contour and depth, poignancy and power, and challenges in loss and grief.

The book in your hands captures the best of what I have learned. It tells a universal human story whose themes thread through the world's great spiritual and religious traditions, even as they weave through our own lives, linking us in our common humanity and shaping our uniqueness.

First, the story tells of how we breathe into life and learn to live in the world and in ties with loved ones in ways we may easily take for granted; next, of how the loss of someone we love takes our breath away as brokenness and sorrow come over us, and then, of how we can catch our breath as we listen to our sorrow, draw upon hope and resilience, relearn how to live in the world, and learn to love in separation.

In this book I invite you to join in wondering about your personal loss, love, and life in the wake of your loved one's last breath, whether it be a parent, spouse or partner, child, other family member, friend, or animal companion. If you come to it while your grief weighs heavily upon you, you may not feel up to accepting this invitation just now. Only you can know when you are ready for this or any other challenge.

When you do feel ready to read, wonder, and reflect, you will likely seek reassurance that your experiences are normal and that you are not alone in having them. May the universality of the story in these pages bring you that comfort.

You will likely also long for something that no general account of grieving can provide: understanding of the uniqueness of your grieving. I regret I cannot be with you to hear all you could tell me. Yet I often address "you" directly because I understand how most, if not all, of the themes in the story I tell will call your attention to details in your story. May its resonance with your experiences enable you to grow in understanding of your own ties with your loved one, loss, and suffering and to find hopeful paths to walk in the next chapters of your life.

By all means read the book in your own way, depending on where you are in grief. You may read it straight through, even all in one sitting – it is brief and simply written, and themes introduced early echo in what comes later. You may begin with the second part to reflect on the depth of your brokenness and sorrow. You may start with the third part to explore ways of moving beyond your suffering and of reengaging in life. Or, because each small piece can stand alone and provide ample food for thought, you may focus on one at a time.

Whatever path you choose, may the book prove a good companion in your wondering over the course of many days, weeks, or months, as you move ahead when you are ready or return to especially compelling pieces as the need arises or your spirit moves you.

And may it help you to
catch your breath in grief.

PART ONE

THE BREATH OF LIFE

*And the Lord God formed man of the dust of the ground,
and breathed into his nostrils the breath of life;
and man became a living soul.*
— Genesis 2:7

*All things share the same breath — the beast, the tree,
the man... the air shares its spirit with all
the life it supports.*
— Chief Seattle

As we take our first breath at birth, the life we know begins. Through all our days, whether we are awake or asleep, breath flows through and sustains us. It animates our bodies, grounds us in a nourishing world, and feeds the fires of our aspirations.

In ordinary experience, breath comes easily. A steady life companion, we take it for granted. Extraordinary experiences take our breath away. Breathless at the peaks, we are beside ourselves in joy. Breathless in the valleys, we are beside ourselves in sorrow. Joy and sorrow remind us that breath is precious.

As we breathe our last at death, the life we know ends.

COMING TO LIFE

*C*oming to life for each of us was amazing: Because two cells, among so many, came together. Because genetic possibilities beyond counting combined to shape a life like no other. Because a miraculous development unfolded in the womb. Because life fulfilled its longing for itself once more.

Dependent on our mothers' breath no longer, we were surrendered into the air and life as we know it. Each first breath was a sacred beginning, a moment set apart and like no other. We drew that breath on our own, though we were still utterly dependent. While we were unaware how extraordinary our coming was, usually others had waited for us, filled with hope. When we took that first breath, it took their breath away. If no one had waited for us, others valued the breath of life in us soon enough, or we would have perished.

Those who welcomed us looked upon us in wonder, asking: "Where were you before this marvelous arrival? Why have you come? Why here and now, and into our lives? What kind of life will your breath support? Who will you become? What meaning and value will your life hold?"

So, too, was your loved one's coming to life remarkable, before or after you came.

LIFE IN THE UNIVERSE

The coming of life in the universe was amazing: Because the universe emerged from silence, a creation from nothingness or an explosion from something no larger than a dot on a page. Because order emerged from chaos. Because Earth formed from stardust with an atmosphere capable of supporting life. Because invisible forces breathed life into inanimate earth, water, air, and fire. And because life's longing for itself burst forth in great abundance.

The coming of life itself was a sacred beginning, a moment set apart and like no other. Whether in real time or mythical time, life in any form was a late arrival. More remarkable still was the eventual coming of human life, a rare and astonishing occurrence in the great scheme of things. How miraculous that you, your loved one, or any other human beings have ever drawn breath!

From its beginning, it was as if the universe had been reaching for meanings and values only life can reveal. As if the coming of life gave birth to joy and wonder. As if the breath of life was a hope of the universe fulfilled.

GRACE

*E*ach of us came to life by the grace of others who conceived and gave us birth, and, ultimately, by a grace of the universe that offers the chance to live meaningfully. As others nurtured us, we learned to give in return.

The breath of life was never anyone's to give. Life has always taken hold within mothers, coming through them until ready to breathe. No one has ever earned or deserved the privileges of birth, nurture to maturity, love, parenting, or the wonders of Earth, including the air that all have breathed since the succession of births began. These have always been gifts.

You may have a name for the something larger that provides these gifts, or you may prefer not to use a name at all. Still, by this wonderful, powerful, life-giving grace of the universe, you came to life, as did your loved one, as did we all.

THE GREAT WEB OF LIFE

Each of us was surrendered into a world teeming with life and sustained by grace. Breath was already coursing through an all-embracing web of life where others welcomed and extended lifelines to us.

This great web emerged through weaving and reweaving of countless lifelines that began with life itself: Air, sun, water, earth, genes, food chains, and ecosystems connecting all living things. Memories, legacies, myths, legends, histories, and traditions binding humanity across time. Paths, highways, waterways, rails, flight patterns, wires, and airwaves spanning distances. Roles, responsibilities, affiliations, competition, cooperation, coordination, customs, moralities, laws, teachings, services, markets, languages, arts, crafts, sciences, and technologies holding society together. Routine, work, give and take, food, music, play, joy, and sorrow threading through daily life. Intimacy, family, friendship, loyalty, care, compassion, love, striving, wisdom, faith, ritual, ceremony, and hope linking souls and spirits.

Energy and life anywhere within this wondrous web ripple through its entire fabric.

LIFE SUPPORT

We are on life support from conception until death. It flows into us along lifelines from our loved ones and the great web of life. Without it, we could not live, grow, or thrive.

At first, our mothers' bodies carry and nourish us. In our early years, others meet our every need. As long as we live, breathing sustains us along central lines to the physical world. As we care about and love one another, we listen for telltale variations in our loved ones' breathing, ready to do all we can to keep it flowing. Vital lifelines to Earth, usually through others, bring water, food, and shelter.

But we always need more than physical life support. Practical, soulful, and spiritual lifelines from our loved ones, family, and larger communities also sustain us. Guidance, training, and assistance support us practically. Nurture, compassion, care, love, and sense of belonging feed our souls. And encouragement, hope, inspiration, wisdom, and understanding fire our spirits.

THE WILL TO LIVE

Deep within, our will to live opens to the grace of the universe, making the best of its offerings. This primal energy of life longing for itself flows silently into and through us from the moment we are conceived, taking only what it needs from our mothers, supporting our growth and development inside them, and reaching for our first breath.

Ordinarily, your will to live keeps you going with the natural ease of your breathing. With you always, it streams effortlessly into the unique opportunities your circumstances afford: As soul, grounding you in meaningful connections with the world around you. And as spirit, propelling you toward value and meaning in change and growth, lifting you to heights and carrying you through depths.

As with breathing, only in stress or crisis do you attend self-consciously to your own or a loved one's will to live, struggling to channel or maintain its flow deliberately through challenges life presents. It is often willing to endure even the harshest conditions, at times seeming indomitable.

Our will to live is instinctive, receptive, grateful, responsive, engaging, patient, persevering, hopeful, enthusiastic, and graceful.

SOUL

Our soul is the home-seeking aspect of our will to live. Like respiration, it grounds us in steady, unself-conscious give and take with the world. We need the secure roots, nourishment, and love our souls find in our mothers' wombs, then in others' care, and eventually wherever we call home.

Your soul breathes into your surroundings, suffusing them with care. The faces, voices, laughter, music, and food of home comfort you. You make special things your own and settle into rooms, neighborhoods, hometowns, and favorite places. Habits and routines anchor you in the familiar. You immerse yourself in daily activities and experiences. You and your loved ones learn of each other's cares, support one another in them, and make some of the others' your own.

You pour your grace, care, and love into ties with loved ones, family, friends, community, animal companions, and nature. You cherish the breath of those closest to you, intimacy and ways of being with them. You touch and make your loved ones and others feel at home, sensing the soul within one another. You find roots in shared histories and traditions. You treasure precious memories and stories of the best in life. Sensing you belong in your surroundings and with your loved ones here and now, you feel at home in the great scheme of things. No wonder traditional belief identifies soul with the breath of life.

SPIRIT

Our spirit is the changing, growing, and striving aspect of our will to live. As aspiration, it quickens as we reach for meaning in the new and extraordinary and rise to challenge. Inspiration motivates and feeds our spirits' fires.

Your spirit stirs in your mother's womb, struggles through birth, and then breathes into your new world, infusing it with energy. Your curiosity, fascination, and adventure weave into the unfamiliar. New things, places, and people excite you. You breathe into novel experiences and activities, sampling fresh delights. Spontaneity and improvisation enliven the everyday. You soar in joy, laughter, surprise, enthusiasm, and ecstasy, especially when you share them with others.

Vision, imagination, and creativity open you to possibility and change. You seek purpose in daily living, to better your lot and strengthen the great web. You strive to grow and become all you can be, pursuing dreams and callings. You move and inspire your loved ones and others, sensing the spirits in one another and in all their energy charges. You and your loved ones come to know each other's aspirations, support one another in them, and make some of the others' your own. Faith, hope, and courage enable you to face and rise above adversity, loss, and suffering. You search for understanding of your place in the great scheme of things. No wonder traditional belief also identifies spirit with breath.

THE WEB OF YOUR LIFE

Within the great web, our souls and spirits breathe into webs of life uniquely our own. Our souls anchor the webs in ties with the great web. Our spirits reweave them in response to growth, change, and challenge.

Your soul weaves a web of lifelines into your daily life pattern. You give, receive, care or love, and are cared about and loved along radiating threads. Wedges of these threads within the web anchor you in richly textured ties with what matters most to you. Your cares and loves affect one another along the connecting threads that bind the wedges together.

Your spirit continuously reweaves this web into your life story. It weaves in new lifelines as your life circumstances change and you mature. And it repairs the web in response to adversity, loss, and suffering.

Together, your soul's cares and loves and your spirit's faith, hope, and courage make you who you are. You find individuality and identity in the unique pattern and history of the weaving of the web of your life. The web embodies your integrity and reflects your character. You come to know the character and uniqueness of your loved ones as your souls and spirits interweave the webs of your lives with one another.

EGO

When we are children, there is "me" and "all the rest." We learn to get what we want, do things our way, solve everyday problems, and compete for attention and advantage. As teens, we long to be somebody; as adults, to make a mark. Others expect and reward individual achievement. We don masks to meet their expectations. Appearance, success, and reputation in their eyes shape our self-image, confidence, and self-esteem. These experiences feed the illusion that we are separate selves, or egos.

Your ego seeks control, defending against perceived threats to this separateness. It stifles awareness of the powerful forces of soul and spirit flowing through you, treating your need, openness, and vulnerability as weaknesses. It fights or flees when it senses danger from without.

The illusion of separateness enables functioning but mistakes it for the whole of your being. Shaken whenever you meet the uncontrollable, the illusion constricts your life, distances and isolates you from loved ones and others, and gives no credit to the depth of your being or theirs. Even as the illusion emerges and takes hold, your soul and spirit anonymously maintain the web of your life and thrive in connection with loved ones, grace, and the great web.

RHYTHMS OF LIFE

Rhythms permeate the universe and life. Our souls breathe into the steady throbbing of life in the familiar; our spirits pulse to the variations of change. The deep rhythms of life in our souls and spirits influence the movements and shape the figures of the dances of our lives.

Your soul attunes to the routine rhythms of waking and sleeping, eating and drinking, coming and going, giving and receiving, habit and routine, speaking and listening, care and love, and intimacy that make you at home in daily life and with your loved ones.

Your spirit lifts you through the extraordinary pulses of growth and development, seasons of life, hardship and striving, adventure and frustration, meeting and parting, hope and despair, joy and sorrow, laughing and crying that change and enrich the course of your life story and permeate life with your loved ones.

Your ego's practical successes keep you upright and in the dance of life. But its self-consciousness and need to control inhibit the flow of the dance and may lead you or your partners to stumble or fall.

DANCING WITH MYSTERY

At its deepest level, life is a dance with mystery. We wonder at the silence that holds everything, the origin of all that is, and our place in the great scheme of things. The meanings of birth, life, and death elude us. The depths of the silence within us, our souls, our spirits, and love awe us. Finiteness, uncertainty, impermanence, imperfection, and suffering shadow us as long as we live.

Constant companions in life, mysteries reveal new aspects of themselves as the dances of our lives unfold. Too important to ignore and too subtle, involving, and enigmatic to comprehend, they maintain a compelling presence through the movements and figures of our years.

Your ego cannot solve, manage, control, fix, or overcome mysteries as if they were everyday practical problems. Instead, your soul and spirit listen for and move in step with the deep rhythms of life and the universe, responding to the changing faces these mysterious partners present. Meanings emerge in the give and take between the needs and grace of your soul and spirit and the demands and grace of the universe.

LOVE

oving another is itself a dance with mystery. We wonder at the breath of life within and compelling presence of each dance partner, whether spouse, life companion, parent, child, friend, or companion animal. The depths of our partners' souls and spirits elude us. The privileges of knowing and being known, loving and being loved, awe us. The meanings of the dance transcend imperfections in the movements and the dancers.

You attune the rhythms of your breathing and lives to one another. You reveal new aspects of yourselves, as your life patterns change, life stories unfold, and characters deepen. Unique and precious meanings emerge in give and take along countless lifelines that unite you. In some figures you are together, in others apart. Your souls and spirits flow into, touch, and affect one another, even when you are physically distant. Your love reveals new aspects as it moves and changes you both through the dance.

Love flows from and into the heart of you. Nothing matters more than the movements and figures you dance with those you love. Joy and sorrow in them take your breath away.

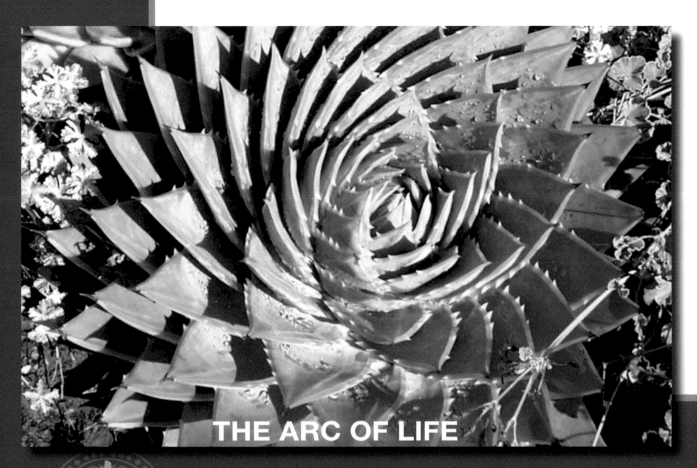

THE ARC OF LIFE

reath traces an arc through our lives from conception to death. It emerges from mystery and silence into utter dependence upon grace and the great web. Through infancy, we receive much and give back relatively little. Our souls connect with life support. Our spirits reach into new surroundings. Our egos barely assert themselves.

As we mature, we breathe more deeply into life. We choose relationships beyond those into which we were born. Our deep identities emerge and our characters bloom as our souls and spirits come into their own. We give more to others in return for all we receive. We rise to responsibility and interdependence. Our egos' focus on selfish wants and reputation blinds us to the depth of our being. Its successes and defensiveness support the illusion that we are completely independent.

In old age, with disabling accidents, or in fatal illness at any point along the arc, we adjust to the decline and failure of our faculties. We return to increased dependence. We may or may not awaken to our souls and spirits. At death, our breath returns to mystery and silence.

LEAVING LIFE

Leaving life can be amazing or awful. Our loved ones survived only as long as they were sustained and protected by health and ego, the will to live within, countless lifelines in the great web, and, ultimately, the grace of the universe. When death came, life's longing for itself had run its earthly course in them.

If they were aware of death's approach, they sensed how extraordinary their leaving would be. You may have anticipated with them, attending to their every breath, filled with sorrow and hope. When their bodies released their last breaths into the air, it took your breath away. If they were unaware, the suddenness or tragedy of their leaving also took your breath away. Their lives unexpectedly cut short, your relationships may seem incomplete, with love, forgiveness, gratitude, and good-byes unspoken. Horror may grip you.

As they have returned to mystery and silence, you wonder: "Where have their precious breath, soul, and spirit gone? Why have they left, or been taken? Why now? Why were they here? How did they touch me so deeply? What meanings do their life stories hold? What of them do I still have in my heart?"

ATTENDING TO BREATH

We can attend to the breath of life through meditation, prayer, retreat, sitting or walking in peaceful places, running or exercising, yoga or the martial arts, communing with nature, singing or chanting, ritual, fellowship, compassion, or while watching over a loved one.

Attending to breath reminds us of all we take for granted. Awakening to the deep flow of soul and spirit within us, we realize that life is so much more than ego having its way. Ties to loved ones and others define us, linking us in soul and spirit. The breath of life flowing through lifelines between us belongs to us and to them. We are who we are because we make differences in one another.

Attending to breath opens us in humility to something larger than our lives, allowing us to resonate with the great, eternal silence that holds the universe and all that comes and goes within it. It attunes us to the rhythms of life and the dance with surrounding mystery, reminding us of where we came from and reconnecting us with the ground of our being in grace.

PART TWO

WHEN LOSS TAKES YOUR BREATH AWAY

*Never does the question of life's meaning and value
arise more urgently and painfully
than when we see the last breath leave a body
that was alive only a moment ago.*
— Carl Jung

oss of someone you love changes your world. It takes your breath away, as if you were punched in the gut, crushed beneath an unbearable weight, or caught in a fierce and devastating storm. Your loss undermines the rhythm and disrupts the momentum of the flow of your life. You haven't actually stopped breathing, but you struggle for air.

Only a moment ago, you breathed into a life that your loved one shared with you. Suddenly, normal breathing is suspended in crisis as brokenness and sorrow come over you. Loss pierces your heart because you were intimately connected to the one you grieve through ties beyond counting in the webs of your lives; you were anything but separate. One day you will breathe fully into life apart. But just now you cannot imagine how. The breath of life persists through crisis, but desperation makes it difficult to sense its resilience deep within.

BREATHTAKING CHANGE

The wake of your loved one's last breath washes over your world. You can easily lose your bearings first in swirling winds of change and then in a fog of suffering: The color and vitality going out of things, places, food, music, events, activities, and experiences. Even those closest to you seeming distant. The flow of daily life breaking down. On one hand, it seeming to you as if chaos has broken out. On the other hand, your resenting the larger world going on as if nothing has happened.

Realizing how much you have taken for granted can easily throw you off balance: Loss unsettling and draining you physically. Your mind flooding with emotions, thoughts, and questions. Your confidence and self-esteem shaken. Wondering who you really are. Not knowing what to do or say. Sensing that your life will never be the same. Your assumptions about the world and your place in it undermined.

Profound change in your world calls for profound change in you. But you are hardly in a position to change while you struggle for breath in the grip of all-encompassing suffering. In crisis, nothing else matters.

BROKENNESS

When your loved one dies, you may sense you are falling apart. Where your loved one anchored your life, loss strikes the web. Penetrating to the center, it threatens the integrity of the web. Reverberating across the web, the blow severs some connecting threads and even dislodges other radiating threads. Lifelines that once found connection dangle. Precious meanings, once sustained along ties to your loved one and others, founder.

Loss shatters any remaining ego illusions. Bad things can happen to you. You are not invulnerable. Your control is limited. You never have been independent. Loss penetrates to the heart of you, unraveling much of your soul's and spirit's weaving and reweaving. It often shatters your daily life pattern and disrupts the flow of your life story. No wonder you ask, "Who am I now?"

You can never be whole again just as you were. To feel whole again, you often have much reweaving to do. But first, your brokenness and sorrow cry for attention. You have every right to retreat from the press of everyday life and dwell in your brokenness while your ego, soul, and spirit are in crisis.

EGO IN CRISIS

Your disillusioned ego may gasp helplessly. It would have been only human to believe you were a separate self. To shrink from vulnerability. And to take for granted a future not yet granted. But your ego was not strong enough to prevent either your loved one's death or the unraveling of your life's web. Nor could it avert sorrow. In crisis, it functions only with difficulty, frustrated and afraid of being overwhelmed.

The famous account of five stages of grief (originally proposed as stages of dying) focuses only on realizing how useless your ego's flight or fight defenses are against death and suffering. Denial retreats from their persistent reality. Anger tries to control the uncontrollable, bargaining to negotiate the unchangeable. Depression concedes the futility of your defenses. And, finally, acceptance grants that death and suffering are real and implicitly acknowledges your ego's limitations.

But accepting the reality of death and suffering does not end effective engagement with them. It only makes it possible. You still need to put your shattered life back together. Your soul and spirit do such weaving and reweaving best. But they, too, are likely in crisis.

SOUL IN CRISIS

Beneath the chaos of your life, your soul may well be in crisis: uprooted, wrenched out of the familiar, homesick, and heaving longingly.

Your soul's anguish may surface in sadness, loneliness, guilt, or anger about ties with your loved one. In insecurity, isolation, or alienation from others. In aching to simply be with your loved one and return to nourishing and sustaining details of life you knew. In doubting you can care so deeply again. Or in wonder if you can ever feel you belong in a world filled with painful reminders of your loved one's absence.

Your soul's sorrow reflects the uniqueness of your love for him or her. No other soul has taken root, settled into the world, or woven a daily life pattern out of threads of deep care and love as yours has. Your troubled soul reveals the shattering effects of loss on your ways of weaving the web of your life and making yourself at home in the world.

SPIRIT IN CRISIS

Beneath the chaos, your spirit may well be in crisis: adrift, fearful, and breathing haltingly.

Your spirit's agony may surface in discouragement, despair, loss of motivation, or loss of faith. In sensing that life may retain no meaning in a world transformed by loss. In wondering if you can overcome sorrow or ever again know hope or joy. In doubting you can face unwelcome change or stretch into an unforeseen future.

No other spirit has motivated, shaped, and guided the unfolding of a life story that reflects deep courage, hope, and desire for meaning as your spirit has. Your spirit's sorrow reflects the uniqueness of the ties of your spirit to your loved one's. And it reveals the disruptive effects of loss on your ways of reweaving the web of your life and finding and making meaning in the life story it holds.

CRISIS SHARED

Rarely do you grieve alone. Your loved one's death unravels the lives of others who grieve with you. They have experienced your loved one differently and know unique agonies. Your sense of their suffering adds to your own.

Longing for the familiar and frightened, your family and community are likely also in crisis, their collective souls heaving and their spirits gasping haltingly.

An irreplaceable presence and central character is missing in family and community life. Loss likely shatters shared daily life patterns and disrupts shared life histories. When your neighborhood in the great web is in tatters, your agony is compounded. And its byways resonate with your sorrow.

Your shared anguish reflects the uniqueness of your collective ties with your loved one. No other family or community has woven a daily life from the same threads of care and love. Nor has any other rewoven a shared life story with the same courage, hope and desire for meaning. Your shared sorrow reveals the shattering effects of loss on the ongoing weaving and reweaving of the webs of family and community life.

SEPARATION

An irreplaceable presence and central character in your daily life and life story is missing. It can be as if absence fouls the air wherever you turn, through day and night, in conscious awareness, and in the depths of your being. If only he or she could be here right now, share another day, or face life with you again!

You probably can't help wishing your loved one still lived. Because he or she no longer lives, the wishing hurts. As does bittersweet nostalgia for life as it was: Bitter because you know you cannot go back. And sweet as you appreciate anew something good about the past.

Often the worst of loss is wanting the one thing you cannot have – the return of the breath of life to the one you love. There is no way to satisfy this fervent longing for the impossible. If it persists and intensifies, it frustrates and immobilizes you. You dwell in a dark place in your heart where missing your loved one consumes you. You want to hold on, but how can you if he or she is not here?

INERTIA

Suffering often has a smothering inertia. When it grips you with its full power, breathlessly you can fear it will never end.

You were unable to control your loved one's death or its cause. You were powerless as brokenness and sorrow came over you. Now you may feel insignificant before forces larger than you, humbled by unchanging mysteries.

Suffering may preoccupy you, filling every moment. It may seem as if you don't merely *have* your suffering, but that you *are* your suffering and nothing more. You may fear that it will never loosen its hold. That nothing you do or say can lead anywhere. That meaning, joy, and love will forever elude you. That you are distant from grace, a victim singled out for arbitrary treatment by a malevolent force that delights in your agony.

When suffering weighs on you so, you can hardly breathe.

VULNERABILITY

While suffering and crisis hold you, vulnerability to further hurt threatens your breathing. The heavier your burdens become, the more likely you will need assistance catching your breath.

You may be reeling from earlier blows, and other blows may come while you are grieving. You may slip from temporary retreat to permanent withdrawal, lingering in denial of reality, clinging to suffering to keep love alive, or adhering to the role of victim to retain others' attention or support.

An inner voice or others may insist you are hopelessly unable to rise above your suffering. Neglect, abandonment, misunderstanding, or criticism may weigh you down. Others may discount your love, loss, or sorrow, even denying your right to grieve. They may expect too much or insist that you grieve "the right way" or "get over it."

Things left unsaid or undone, negative ties, or serious troubles with your loved one may preoccupy you. Or horror in the circumstances of his or her death may further burden your breathing with trauma.

RESILIENCE

An amazing resilience abides within you. Beneath brokenness and crisis, the breath of life persists. Your will to live, soul, spirit, and love are not broken. The more easily you open to their life-sustaining flow, the more likely you will again breathe fully into life.

Much of value in the tattered web of your life remains intact. And much good in the great web that holds all life still supports, or streams within reach of, your body, soul, and spirit.

Loss does not extinguish your will to live. Breath still animates your body. Your soul can still find sustenance in familiar surroundings; draw from roots in family, community, history, and tradition; care and love deeply; and find grounding in the great scheme of things. Your spirit can still find hope, faith, and courage to rise above suffering; stretch into the new and unknown; change and grow; seek understanding; and know joy again. And the love still pulsing in you can cherish precious memories and lasting legacies, revive connections with fellow survivors, and open to new relationships.

PART THREE

CATCHING
YOUR BREATH

Although our world is full of suffering,
it is full also of the overcoming of it.
— Helen Keller

*Y*ou catch your breath as you revive the will to live, soul, and spirit that breathed into life when you were born. As they breathe into life again, these aspects of your deep self reweave your life's web and heal your sorrow.

Loss and suffering happen to you. Suffering's intensity stifles the flow of your breathing. But sorrow holds you motionless for a reason. When you give it the attention it cries for, learning what it tells you about the crises in, and deepest needs of, your soul and spirit, your breathing eases.

Grieving is what you do with your loss and suffering. Reweaving your life requires effort in the midst of sorrow. As you draw on the resilience within and reconnect with vital lifelines and grace in the great web, you reach through suffering and willingly surrender to life again.

The effort of active grieving restores rhythm and momentum to your breathing. It does not bring closure on either missing or loving the one you grieve. But you learn to carry the pain of missing your loved one, relearn the world of your experience, and find ways of loving in separation.

MEETING BASIC NEEDS

While you struggle to catch your breath, you realize you won't be yourself for a while. It helps to collect yourself to protect against further blows, retreat from life, and keep things simple. Meeting basic needs will steady your breathing.

Attending to breath tames the chaos within and readies you for dialogue with your deep self. Tending to your body's needs for food, water, rest, comfort, and touch provide home maintenance for your soul and spirit. Expecting less of yourself, deflecting others' demands, taking time out, delaying major decisions, and calming and soothing yourself restore your soul and spirit. Accepting or asking for help you need, spending time with people who care about you, connecting with the best in life, and awakening to wonder and mystery reestablish a habitat for your humanity.

These small steps begin engagement with the unraveling of the web of your life. Minimal effort relieves your ego's helplessness. Kindness to yourself revives your caring soul. And sensing prospects revives your hopeful spirit.

BREATHING INTO SORROW

reathing into your sorrow deepens your breath, replenishing your soul,
and awakening your spirit. Respecting sorrow, you affirm its depth and
value. Neither resisting nor fleeing from it, you welcome its flow. Giving it
attention, you trust it to guide your reweaving. Entering into dialogue with
en and probe. Opening to insights about being, living, and meaning, you
ow to become whole again.

hing into sorrow is soulful, making you at home with your deep self.
eciate subtler aspects of your being and dwell compassionately with your
You explore what matters most in connections, cares, loves, and your loved
You wonder how to live more gratefully.

hing into sorrow is spiritual, meaning-seeking, and hopeful. You venture
fe's surface, looking for healing and growth in deep currents within. You go
logue with sorrow leads and open to new ways of living.

 you breathe into it, sorrow loosens its grip. You expand beyond your ego's
s and breathe more deeply into the fullness of your being and the world
ed by your loss.

LISTENING TO EMOTION

Listening to your emotions is a way of breathing into sorrow, reaching past the hurt in them to hear what they are about. When you take to heart what they tell you, they help you catch your breath.

The word "emotion" means "without motion." When emotions come over you or tears, moans, screams, shivers, gestures, or words pour out of you, your life stands still. Like physical pains, emotional pains hold you motionless for good reason. You ignore or stifle them at your peril. More than expression, they cry for understanding. And they persist until you pay attention.

When you attend to them, your emotions tell you about brokenness, all you've taken for granted, and what you need for survival, reweaving your life's web, and thriving. Your ego's emotions speak about its needs to be effective and its illusions of separateness and control. Your soul's emotions tell about its needs for roots, belonging, nurture, connection, care and love. And your spirit's emotions speak about its needs for courage, hope, purpose, meaning, adventure, and joy. When heard and understood, your emotions loosen their paralyzing grip and begin motivating tentative actions of healing and new growth.

USING SORROW-FRIENDLY PRACTICES

your extraordinary life experiences of loss and suffering call for extraordinary responses. You may know your soul and spirit well, drawing upon them instinctively as you respond to what has happened. Or you may do well to use sorrow-friendly practices to learn from your sorrow, discerning stifled aspects of your soul or spirit.

Sorrow-friendly practices teach you to breathe into the fullness of life: Taking you away from the everyday. Allowing sorrow to surface and flow freely. Enabling you to listen to your emotions. Supporting dialogue with your deep self. And yielding valuable lessons about reweaving your web and reestablishing your place in the great web.

Sorrow-friendly practices include using ceremony or ritual, sharing and exploring sorrow with another, keeping a grief journal, meditating, attending to sorrow in your body, catching dreams, engaging with unconscious images, seeking meaning in after-death encounters with your loved one, experiencing or creating works of art, surrendering in silence to mystery, attending to breath, leaning into faith, or opening your heart in prayer.

CHOOSING LIFE

You choose to live again by finding the courage to be despite your brokenness and sorrow. Deep within, your grieving soul and spirit call you to resist the inertia of suffering and resume weaving and reweaving your life.

Your resilient soul cries, "Despite losing so much grounding of my life's meaning, it is worth living here and now. I feel a powerful impulse to connect, care deeply, and cherish offerings, gifts, and blessings too precious to ignore. I want to make myself at home in life again, weaving together its tattered threads. Too much goodness can still be mine. I will push through the debris around me to reclaim and embrace enduring meanings."

And your resilient spirit cries, "Despite the undoing of so much of my life's prospect, it is worth entering the unknown future. I feel a powerful impulse to say yes to abiding grace and what is yet to be. I will rise above what only appears to be defeat. I want to make the best of unwelcome change and reweave the web of my life. Too many possibilities remain open. I will feel the fear but reach for meaning and value anyway."

REACHING THROUGH HURT

Wherever you turn, you miss your loved one. Photos, gifts, mementoes, things, furnishings, food, music, places, occasions, activities, experiences, family members, friends, even your own reflection in the mirror, gestures, habits, or character remind you of your separation.

First encounters with painful reminders occur only once. Fewer occur as time passes. But you never finish having them. And even the familiar can arouse fresh pain. You will always hold the one you grieve in a sad place in your heart where you miss him or her. Gradually, you can grow accustomed to sadness in the air and learn to carry the pain of being apart.

But in reminders you also meet something touched by your loved one or from your life together. Reaching through your hurt, you can reconnect with him or her: Finding enduring meanings in your surroundings, ways of being who you are, and companion memories. Savoring remembered life again, the continuing presence of your loved one's soul and spirit, and love revived. Tempering longing for an impossible return, missing your loved one as you did when apart, and even smiling through your tears.

BEING RESOURCEFUL

*B*eing resourceful is vital to success in catching your breath and coming back to your life. As the fog of suffering recedes ever so slightly, it is easier to recognize that through the worst of grief vital lifelines from the great web are still in place supporting you. When you tap into what they offer, you take in nourishment for a return to thriving that feeds your body, supports practical life, welcomes you home, bolsters your courage, and arouses your hope.

You may find life support in familiar settings or routines, with friends or family members, in grief support groups, from volunteer or professional caregivers, or in stories of others overcoming suffering.

The heartfelt desires of your loved one for you can be an especially valuable resource. More than likely, he or she wanted you to cherish memories, but break free of the inertia of suffering, return to living meaningfully, and make the best of his or her legacies.

COMING BACK TO YOUR LIFE

Coming back to your life is like coming into the fullness of life when you were born. You begin, hesitantly at first, to breathe again into the abundance in the great web.

You have not reverted to infancy. But you are likely withdrawn and not ready to fully engage in the weaving and reweaving life requires. Emerging from crisis is an extraordinary transition. Others who care about you wait for you, again full of hope. You wonder what meaning and value life yet holds for you. How remarkable that life still longs for itself in you!

Hope disposes you to reweave constructively and live well in the world your loved one left behind. But caution says to begin with small steps when you feel ready and to pace yourself carefully. Small steps include things you can say or do now to begin to embrace the good that remains. To mend your brokenness. To reenter daily life. To reach out and reconnect. To change familiar but unhappy ways of living and open yourself to alternatives. And to attune yourself to offerings of the moment, others, and grace.

BEING HOPEFUL

Hope eases suffering's constriction and quickens your pulse. It opens you to and reaches for the possible. It feeds your impulses to overcome suffering, weave your way back into life, care and love, and find meaning. In hope you envision possibilities that you would welcome and take positive steps toward realizing them.

Hope is not expectation. Expectation presumes to know what will happen and takes for granted what has not yet been granted. Hope is not wishing. Wishing focuses on what is beyond reach, resigns to harsh realities, and waits for something to happen. Hope strives humbly in uncertainty and is receptive to grace. It desires goodness fully, dissolves passivity, perseveres, and nurtures that goodness, even in life's shadows.

In hope you welcome and strive for the best in life: enduring meanings in the familiar, daily purpose, connections with others, memories, legacies, adventure, growth, transformation, joy, grace, and a sense of belonging in the great scheme of things.

REVIVING EGO

Your ego breathes into practical functioning again. With modest successes, your confidence and self-esteem return.

Using lessons from ego pain wisely enables you to trust your ego again to do what it does best. You make small decisions first and bigger ones only when you are ready. You start to face and solve everyday problems. You resume control of what is yours to control. And, gradually, you return to navigating effectively in practical life.

Greater awareness of the depth of your being and interdependence within the great web enables you to resist your ego's tendencies to illusion and overreaching: You are not separate and self-sufficient. You are not entitled to control events or others or to insist your suffering hold center stage at their expense. Life is more than appearance, success, and reputation. Defensiveness obscures your deep needs and isolates you from others. And attempting to fix mysteries, as if they were problems, is futile.

REVIVING SOUL

Your soul breathes into and makes itself at home again in the familiar. You find grounding and sustenance in renewed give and take with the world in figures and movements of the dance of life you know well.

Using lessons from soul pain wisely returns you to living again with soul. You weave still intact lifelines into a web of daily life that will likely only resemble what it was when your loved one lived. You settle back into your surroundings. You test and trust again what remains meaningful in familiar activities, experiences, routines, habits, and life patterns. You revive viable daily purposes, projects, hopes, and dreams. You draw nourishment and support from roots already in place. You pour your care and love again into familiar ways of being with surviving loved ones, family, friends, community, animal companions, and nature. You make yourself at home in the new shape of daily life and the next chapters of your life story as your spirit stretches into them. And you feel grateful for the grace of the universe.

REVIVING SPIRIT

Your spirit breathes into new challenges and possibilities for adventure, value, and joy. You change, grow, and stretch into new meanings in life. Using lessons from spirit pain wisely enables you to live with spirit again. You reweave the web of your daily life, joining new threads with the familiar. You reach past your hurt and enter the unknown with courage, faith, and hope. You give your life new direction and purpose. You open to new connections with others, including to the one you grieve. You embrace offerings of grace as they present themselves. You learn new figures and movements in the dance of your life. Your energy flows again through curiosity, fascination, and delight, into creativity, spontaneity, joy, laughter, surprise, enthusiasm, and ecstasy. You find and make fresh meanings in the next chapters of your life story.

Through loss and sorrow you may develop new strength of character: As you grow in self-understanding and appreciation of your soul and spirit. As you become more sensitive and responsive to others. As you learn how much others mean to you and new ways to show gratitude and love. Or as you gain critical perspective on reality and life in the human condition.

GIVING BACK

You breathe still more fully into life as you begin to give as well as receive along lifelines of connection to others and the great web. Giving back returns you to the more balanced give and take of normal breathing.

When loss takes your breath away and suffering absorbs your energy, you depend on others giving to you. You may want to give in return, but are hardly able. You struggle to take in what you can along lifelines others extend to you. Only later, as your soul and spirit revive, are you able to give back to others, in small ways at first, along those same lifelines.

You come back to life by expressing gratitude for kindness. Appreciating more than ever the depth of others' suffering and offering compassion and support. Returning care and love to family and friends. Rededicating yourself to doing your part to sustain ties with others. And contributing in daily life and giving again to something larger than you are.

REWEAVING YOUR LIFE

ogether, your soul's cares and loves, and your spirit's faith, hope, and courage reweave the web of your life, blending the old with the new. Your web's new pattern and history support a new identity, embody a new integrity and reflect changes in your character. Reweaving heals your brokenness and enables the breath of life to flow more easily through the lifelines of the web.

Reweaving changes the patterns of the threads of your caring connections to things, places, experiences, and activities, other individuals, family, and community. It takes your life story in new directions, changing its plot, sub-plots, and themes as well as roles that you, fellow survivors, and newcomers play. And it changes the choreography of the dance of life that courses along the threads of the web, its rhythms, steps, movements, solo figures, and figures with others.

REWEAVING WITH OTHERS

You join others who grieve with you in reweaving the webs of family and community life, again blending the old with the new. Joint reweaving heals collective brokenness and enables the breath of life to flow more easily along lifelines that bind you together.

You cannot help being affected by one another's sorrows, struggles, memories, interpretations, and success or failure in reweaving your individual webs. The quality of give and take between you affects how well you blend your cares, loves, faiths, courage, and hopes in reweaving the webs of shared life. As you reweave with others, you find and create new ways of being together. You change patterns of caring connection among you, courses of family and community histories, and the dances along lifelines that weave your lives together.

LOVING IN SEPARATION

Nothing is more essential to catching your breath than continuing to dance in separation. Your loved one's life, soul, and spirit still move you. Reweaving memories and legacies – the enduring rewards of your relationship – into the web of your life makes you whole again.

You spend most waking hours apart from those you love when they are alive. You think about, remember, talk about, and pray for them. You share their interests, concerns, hopes, and dreams. You appreciate, model yourself after, keep commitments to, and draw inspiration from them. Sometimes you laugh; sometimes you cry. You know well these ways of the heart.

In the heart of grief, you continue in all these ways when your loved one dies. You reweave threads of enduring connection with him or her into the web of your life. You develop themes of lasting love and give your loved one a new place in the next chapters of your life story. And you sustain some of the music, rhythms, and movements of loving and being loved in the next figures of the dance of your life.

LETTING GO

eath does mean letting go of your loved one's physical presence and missing all it made possible. But the dance of love continues in separation. And you will always hold your loved one in your heart in bright places where you cherish precious memories and legacies.

Anger or guilt about troubles with your loved one may fill other darker places in your heart. You breathe more easily into loving in separation when you let go of them, too, sometimes with great difficulty. Forgiving is a way of letting go. You allow your loved one to be as he or she truly is. You accept your own human failings. And you let your life together be what it was.

Forgiveness reaches past trouble and imperfection to enduring value and meaning. It frees you to appreciate how you are better for your loving. And to resolve to continue dancing in separation in ways that enrich your life.

Perhaps you can let go of lesser troubles easily. But you may need support from someone who listens well or offers wise counsel to disentangle yourself from serious troubles.

REMEMBERING

As the fog of sorrow clears, your loved one returns to you in ever more vivid memory. Remembering enriches the air you breathe with some of the best of life. You do not retreat to the past, linger with an image in your head, or dwell on separation. Here and now you attend to, are moved by, and love the one you remember.

Your loved one's life story interweaves with your own, your family's, and your community's stories. Loving through memory continues the interweaving. Values and meanings in your loved one's life permeate yours. Memories of a story like no other give life to your life.

Revisiting the story, alone or with others, deliberately or spontaneously, returns new rewards each time. You recall different details, reinterpret meanings, and deepen your appreciation of the delights, narrative threads, character, mystery, and life lessons the story holds.

Remembering gives your loved one a renewed vital presence in your life. Still dancing in separation, you may admire, respect, praise, or forgive him or her, feeling the warmth of your love while sensing his or hers.

EMBRACING LEGACIES

Y ou breathe into more of the best of life when you embrace your loved one's legacies. Their gifts are with you and in you every day.

You realize that you took much for granted when he or she lived. No matter how often you said thank you, you could not have captured all he or she gave. So much between you took place beneath your awareness as your souls and spirits flowed into one another.

You may be grateful for precious material legacies, even genetic inheritances. But, more deeply, you can appreciate ways your loved one influenced how you live, shaped your character, and inspired you. You still meet him or her in your ways of doing things. In your soul's ways of making you at home in your daily living, caring, and loving. And in your spirit's ways of stretching into the new and finding meaning in your life story.

You are already a living legacy. You may at any time strive to be more like the one you grieve. Or one day be changed again by his or her soul or spirit as you open to a life lesson you once resisted.

RETURNING HOME IN THE UNIVERSE

As you recover the rhythm and momentum of your breathing, you come to trust again the source of life and all that is.

Rarely, if ever, did you question your beliefs when life was going well. Reexamining, deepening, or changing beliefs may help you better understand your place in the great scheme of things. Spiritual practices such as meditation, prayer, worship, walking in silence, music, communing with nature, or compassion may give you an immediate sense of grounding in something larger than yourself.

But there is no more direct way to return home in the universe than to again pour your soul and spirit into living satisfyingly and meaningfully: Into your corner of the great web. And into the fullness of life it supports. Just as you did when you first came to life.

You will feel at home in the universe when you catch your breath in grief, open again to the wonder of life, and give places in your heart to your loved one and the full range of cares, loves, and hopes that make you who you are.

BEING GRATEFUL

Y ou breathe most deeply into life when you accept heartache as the price of love. You would not hurt so much had you not been given a unique place in the great web of life, a life to live, soul and spirit with which to live it, and the privilege of loving and being loved by the one you grieve. The pain of missing him or her is an inevitable companion to the joy of his or her sharing life with you.

Avoiding love out of fear of sorrow would have cost you all you miss. And allowing fear to control you as you enter the next chapters of life would cost you all you still have.

When you realize your good fortune in having your loved one in your life, an amazing grace assures you that courage, hope, and joy outweigh fear, despair, and sorrow. You live more fully when you are grateful.

CONTINUING THE DANCE

Your soul and spirit continue dancing with mystery. Meanings still emerge in the deep rhythms of give and take between the needs and grace of your soul and spirit and the demands and grace of others and the universe.

Nothing matters more to you than movements and figures you dance with those you love, including the one you grieve, fellow survivors, and others who come to mean something to you as life continues.

The dance unfolds smoothly again when you move past ego illusion that impoverishes life. When you breathe into sorrow, take its wisdom to heart, and draw upon your healing strength to overcome it. When you open to the grace that still provides the wonders of existence, life, love, memory, and legacy. When you allow your soul and spirit to respond trustingly, confidently, and gratefully. And when you realize how life is richer when you are fully present in the moment, giving to something larger than your self, and loving, even in separation.

Perhaps your soul and spirit will breathe into the mysteries of another life or way of living when the breath you draw on Earth falls silent.

ACKNOWLEDGMENTS

Thanks to the grace of the universe that opened me to life as it comes, the flow of soul and spirit within, and dialogue with others. That enabled me to learn and grow through my own and shared experiences of mystery, loss, sorrow, hope, and love. And that provided whatever clarity, image, and insight that have found their way into these pages.

And thanks to the grace of others: The generosity of grieving people who poured their stories, souls, and spirits into me. The fine aesthetic sense and laughing spirit of my life-long friend, Bill Rathje, who soulfully matched his exquisite photos to my words. The keen eye and deft touch of Marsha Batchelor who added her design to this book. The loyalty, care, abiding enthusiasm, and patience of my dear friend, Don Scherer, and wife, Betty Davies, who guided me through several drafts. And the friendship and support for this labor of love from Bill McMillen, Mal and Di McKissock, Paul Rosenblatt, Jeffrey Kauffman, Chuck Corr, Earl Grollman, Sandy Bertman, Ira Byock, Bill Worden, Nancy Murray, Nancy Hogan, Danai Papadatou, Joy Johnson, Darcy Harris, Sister Francis Dominica, Terrie Rando, Sherry Schachter, Bob Neimeyer, Ten Rynearson, Bob Fulton, Bill Lamers, Kath Murray, and Bruce Batchelor.

ABOUT THE AUTHOR

Thomas Attig, PhD, is an applied philosopher and author of *How We Grieve: Relearning the World* (Revised edition, 2011) and *The Heart of Grief: Death and the Search for Lasting Love* (2000), both with Oxford University Press. A Past President of the Association for Death Education and Counseling and recipient of the *Lifetime Achievement Award* from The International Network on Personal Meaning, Tom now lives in Victoria, British Columbia where he continues writing and teaching on-line. He invites you to visit his web site at www.griefsheart.com.

ABOUT THE PHOTOGRAPHER

William Rathje, PhD (1945–2012), was a renowned archaeologist best known for *The Garbage Project*, using archaeological methods to mine landfills for insight into contemporary culture. His photos appeared in *National Geographic*, *Natural History*, and *Shambala Sun*. He photographed the natural world to provide vivid emotional connections with the assimilation of life's ups and downs. See *Remembering Bill* at www.griefsheart.com.

CPSIA information can be obtained
at www.ICGtesting.com
Printed in the USA
LVIC04n0108210315
431470LV00002B/3

* 9 7 8 0 9 8 8 0 7 6 0 1 3 *